YOU CHOOSE

CAN YOU SUCCEED ON AN EPIC NORSE ADVENTURE?

An Interactive Mythological Adventure

by Bruce Berglund

COMPASS POINT BOOKS
a capstone imprint

Published by Capstone Press, an imprint of Capstone
1710 Roe Crest Drive North Mankato, Minnesota 56003
capstonepub.com

Copyright © 2023 by Capstone. All rights reserved. No part of this publication may be reproduced in whole or in part, or stored in a retrieval system, or transmitted in any form or by any means, electronic, mechanical, photocopying, recording, or otherwise, without written permission of the publisher.

Library of Congress Cataloging-in-Publication Data is available
on the Library of Congress web site.
ISBN 9781666337846 (library binding)
ISBN 9781666337853 (paperback)
ISBN 9781666337860 (ebook PDF)

Summary: Thor and Loki have a complicated relationship. The two enjoy going on grand adventures, but they are often at odds with each other. Thor is a strong and brave warrior, while Loki uses his quick wits to outsmart his enemies. But Loki also enjoys playing tricks on Thor to make him look foolish. Which of these famous characters from Norse mythology will you choose to be? Will you be able to avoid getting into trouble? The choices YOU make will determine if the people of Asgard think of you as a hero—or a fool.

Editorial Credits
Editor: Aaron Sautter; Designer: Bobbie Nuytten; Media Researcher: Morgan Walters; Production Specialist: Polly Fisher

All internet sites appearing in back matter were available and accurate when this book was sent to press.

Table of Contents

About Your Adventure 5

Chapter 1
A New Adventure Begins 7

Chapter 2
Loki's Devious Tricks 15

Chapter 3
Adventure in the Land of Ogres..... 43

Chapter 4
Journey to Giantland.................67

Chapter 5
The God of Thunder
and the Trickster 103

    Norse Family Tree 106

    Other Paths to Explore 108

    Bibliography 109

    Glossary................................ 110

    Read More............................. 111

    Internet Sites.......................... 111

    About the
Author 112

About Your Adventure

More than 1,000 years ago, people from Scandinavia were known as the Norse. They believed in and worshipped many gods. Two of them appear often in Norse myths. Thor, the god of thunder, was brave and strong. Loki, the god of mischief, was clever and enjoyed playing tricks. They had fun going on adventures together. But Loki's tricks often caused problems for Thor.

Chapter One sets the scene. Then you choose which path to take. Follow the directions at the bottom of each page. The choices you make determine what will happen next. After you finish your path, go back and read the others for more adventures.

YOU CHOOSE the path you take through this mythical adventure.

The gods often feasted together with the honored dead in Odin's great hall of Valhalla.

Chapter 1
A New Adventure Begins

The gods of Asgard are feasting in a great hall lit with candles. The room is loud with talking and laughter. At one end of the room, seated in the place of honor is Odin, the All-father.

He has a long gray beard and the robes of a wise ruler. A patch covers one eye, and two ravens sit on the back of his chair. Each day, the ravens fly off to Midgard, the world of humans, and report what they see to Odin.

Thor is easy to spot with his long hair and beard. He's not too handsome. But he is big and strong, with thick forearms and broad shoulders. Clearly, he is the strongest of the gods.

Turn the page.

Loki is sitting next to Thor. Loki is actually a giant, rather than a god. But he is smaller than most giants, and he even looks slender next to the mighty Thor.

The two of them are enjoying goblets of wine and plates of food. Thor is feasting on a mountain of meat piled before him. Loki eats quickly and then gets back to talking.

"You have to remember, Thor," says Loki, "I never mean any harm when I play my tricks. I'm only having fun. You're always tromping around, fighting giants and acting tough. Sometimes you need to loosen up."

"I admit it, Loki," Thor answers, wiping some wine from his moustache. "I do laugh at your tricks. But only after I threaten to rip off your arms.

"Maybe we should go on a new adventure," Thor continues, waving an ox rib at Loki. "It's springtime. The snow has melted, and the sun is shining. After being inside all winter, it would be nice to get out and stretch the muscles. Maybe knock some giants' heads together."

"You do the head knocking," Loki answers. "I'll use mine to trick them instead." Loki taps a finger on his head, reminding his friend that he uses his brain while Thor uses his biceps.

"Wonderful!" says Thor. "We'll set off tomorrow. My chariot will be ready in the morning."

> To play a trick on Thor as Loki, turn to page 10.
>
> To be Thor and prepare for a new adventure, turn to page 12.

Thor finishes off his cooked rib and downs the last of his wine. He gives you a friendly slap on the back. You hate when Thor does that. He doesn't know his own strength, and his friendly slaps always hurt.

"Loki, my friend," says Thor. "I look forward to a new adventure with you. But right now, I'm going to dance with my beautiful wife. I'll see you tomorrow."

"Yes, bright and early," you say, lifting your goblet.

You watch Thor dance with his wife, Sif. Thor's right—she is very beautiful. She is graceful and kind, with long golden hair. In the hall's candlelight, you see the glimmer of her wedding ring. Thor had it made from the red gold of the dwarves.

"Thor doesn't deserve a wife as beautiful as Sif," you grumble. "He's a big, ugly brute."

"Another adventure," you sigh, taking another drink of wine. "How boring. Thor's adventures always end up the same. He just gets in fights and breaks stuff."

You look again at Thor and Sif. They're laughing as they spin to the music.

"Maybe it would be good to play a trick on them," you mumble to yourself. "Just a little one to liven things up."

You think it over for a bit, and an idea soon comes to you. You know just the trick to play on the happy couple. You lift your goblet toward Thor and Sif with a smile and then gulp down the last of your wine.

Turn to page 15.

You gobble down the last chunk of meat from your ox rib and then take a big drink from your wine goblet. You look at Loki's empty plate.

"Did you even eat anything?" you ask.

"I eat quickly," answers Loki. "You know that."

"Oh, yes. It leaves your mouth free for more talking," you say. "Well, I need my rest if we're going on an adventure tomorrow. I'll see you in the morning."

"Bright and early," says Loki, lifting his goblet and flashing his mischievous smile. You wonder if he's already planning something.

You make your way back to your chamber. A night of wine and feasting has made you sleepy. Your wife, Sif, is already there, brushing her long golden hair.

"Did you have fun with Loki?" Sif asks as you kiss her cheek.

"Yes, we had many laughs!" you answer. "We remembered the time we tricked some dwarves out of their gold. We're leaving early tomorrow to see what new adventures we can find."

"Where are you planning to go?" Sif asks, as you tuck yourself into bed.

"Good question," you say. You smile at the thought of a trip with Loki. "Where shall we go?"

> To visit the land of the ogres, turn to page 43.
>
> To journey to the land of the giants, turn to page 67.

In many Norse tales, Loki often disguises himself to play tricks on the gods.

Chapter 2
Loki's Devious Tricks

It's late at night, and the great hall is quiet. Thor and Sif had a long night of dancing. Then they left for their own hall called Birskirnir, which means Sound of Lightning.

You are the only one awake in Asgard. Even Odin's ravens are asleep. You sneak to the great iron door of Birskirnir and slowly push it open. Thor never locks his door.

"Who would dream of stealing from the mighty Thor? Only someone like me," you snicker to yourself as you sneak inside.

> To steal Sif's wedding ring, turn to page 16.
> To steal Thor's food, turn to page 19.

You tiptoe across the huge room where Thor welcomes his guests. You've feasted with Thor here many times. Even in the dark, you know your way past the wooden chairs and tables.

Eventually, you reach the stairs that go up to Thor and Sif's chamber. You climb the stairs quietly, careful not to make the slightest sound. You reach the top and find yourself at the end of a long, long hallway with hundreds of doors.

You remember Thor bragged to you about how big Birskirnir is. "It's even bigger than Odin's hall," he told you. "It has 540 rooms."

But you know Thor well. You open the first door. Sure enough, Thor and Sif are sleeping soundly inside.

"Good thing Thor sleeps close to the stairs," you whisper to yourself. "He likes an easy trip to the kitchen when he wants a late-night snack."

You sneak into the room and creep to the sleeping couple's bed. On the right side, under all the quilts, is an enormous, snoring lump. That's Thor.

You go to the other side where Sif is sleeping peacefully. She's facing toward you, with her left hand on her pillow. There, shining in the moonlight, is her ring of red gold.

This will be a challenge, you think. *I'd better disguise myself.*

With a wave of your hand, you change into a mouse and climb onto Sif's pillow. Carefully, you grab hold of her ring with your front paws and start pulling.

The ring slides up her finger, but then stops at the joint. You gently tug on the ring, careful not to pull too hard. But you don't notice that your long whiskers are tickling Sif's nose.

Turn the page.

Suddenly, Sif reaches her hand up to brush her nose, sending you flying off the bed. You hear Sif's covers rustle as she brushes the itch on her nose and rolls over. Thankfully, she doesn't wake up.

You change back to your natural form and peer over the edge of the bed. Now Sif is sleeping with her back to you. Her hands are tucked too close to that snoring lump, Thor.

Now what do I do? you wonder to yourself.

You see Sif's long golden hair spread over the pillow. "Ah-ha," you whisper. "That could be an even better trick. Or maybe I should just steal Thor's food."

> To sneak into the kitchen, go to page 19.
> To steal Sif's golden hair, turn to page 21.

You quietly sneak back to the large room where Thor holds feasts for the other gods of Asgard. You've been here many times. You know that the kitchen is in the back. You open the wooden door quietly. Thor's servants sleep near the kitchen. You don't want to wake them.

Stepping carefully, you make your way across the kitchen's stone floor to the larder where Thor's meat and ale are stored. You're surprised to find a heavy iron lock on the door.

Turn the page.

"Who leaves their palace gate open but locks up their food?" you ask yourself.

You pull at the lock and lean over to look in the keyhole. "There must be a key here somewhere," you say, as you search the kitchen. But it's not in the drawers, on the shelves, or hanging from any hooks.

You have many talents, but picking locks is not one of them. "My trick will have to wait for another night," you grumble to yourself.

You sneak back out through the main hall and the iron gate. Your plan has failed this time. But you know you'll get Thor another time.

THE END

To follow another path, turn to page 9.
To learn more about Thor and Loki, turn to page 103.

The next morning, you hear Thor's voice roaring all the way across Asgard.

"Loki!"

You roll over in bed with a smile on your face. "Sounds like Thor has discovered my trick," you say to yourself.

"LOKI!!!"

His voice is getting louder—and closer. Thor must be on his way to your palace.

"I'd better get ready to meet my guest," you say as you get out of bed. When Thor stomps through your door, you're washed, dressed, and charmingly handsome as ever.

"What did you do to Sif's hair?" Thor yells. He grabs your collar and lifts you off the ground.

"What happened to Sif's hair?" you ask in a raspy voice.

Turn the page.

"You *know* what happened," Thor growls. "It's gone—all of it. Instead of long golden hair, she has a pink, bald head. She's sobbing. Why did you cut it off?"

"I didn't cut it off," you explain, snickering. "I took it off by the roots. She'll go through life with a pink, bald head."

"No, she won't!" Thor yells, lifting you higher. "You're going to put her hair back!"

"But I can't put her hair back," you insist. "It doesn't work that way."

"You'd better figure out a way to get it back," Thor says with a growl. "Or else I'll break every bone in your body."

Thor grabs your pinkie finger with his other hand and starts to crush it. The pain is unbearable.

"The dwarves can do it!" you blurt. "The dwarves can get her hair back!"

"Then you'd better go see the dwarves," he says, dropping you to the floor. You gasp for breath and rub your aching finger.

"I'll be waiting," Thor says, pointing his thick finger in your face. Then he turns and leaves.

It was only a prank, you think. *But maybe I went too far.*

You quickly lace up your magic shoes that allow you to run across the sky. Then you fly off to Svartálfheim, where the dwarves live.

Your shoes bring you swiftly to the workshop of three dwarves called the sons of Ivaldi. Everyone knows they're the best craftsmen among the dwarves.

Turn the page.

You find the dwarves inside their cave by their forge. They're sitting quietly, enjoying their pipes and tankards of ale. They're friendly dwarves and greet you warmly. You explain the reason for your visit, without revealing how Sif lost her hair.

"Only the sons of Ivaldi can spin gold as fine as hair," you say. "And only you can give that gold the magic to grow on Sif's head."

"This is true," says one dwarf. "Our magic can restore Sif's golden hair. But what do we get in return?"

"You'll have the thanks of Thor and Sif and the friendship of the gods. And I'll pledge my services to you whenever you need them," you say.

"The first two rewards have great value," says another dwarf, glancing at you. "The third, not so much. But we'll do this. Thor's gratitude and the friendship of the gods will be useful in the future."

The sons of Ivaldi then build a blazing fire in their forge and begin their work. One dwarf takes molten gold from the forge, another cools and hammers it, and the third spins it into strands as fine as hair.

You marvel as they work. The golden hair is certainly worthy of Sif's beauty. Thor will be pleased. The dwarves' talents could be useful to you. Perhaps you could use that to your advantage.

> To play a trick on the sons of Ivaldi, turn to page 26.
>
> To take the hair back to Thor, turn to page 29.

"You know what I've heard, sons of Ivaldi?" you ask. "Some say that Brokk and Eitri are the greatest craftsmen among the dwarves."

"That's a lie," says the dwarf spinning the gold. "Look at this gold. It's as fine as silk. We'll say a magic spell over it, so it will grow on Sif's head. Those knuckleheads Brokk and Eitri couldn't do anything like this."

"Well, they say their treasures are better than yours," you reply. "I hear they've challenged you to make three treasures for the gods. They'll also make three treasures, and then the gods will choose whose are the best."

The sons of Ivaldi laugh. "That's a challenge we'll win easily," says the one working the forge. "Go tell those boneheads we accept."

You leave and race across the sky to the cave of Brokk and Eitri. These dwarves aren't as friendly.

"What do you want, trickster?" says Brokk.

"I come as a messenger," you say. "The sons of Ivaldi say they are better craftsmen than you. They called you boneheads."

"Boneheads?" says Eitri.

"Yes, boneheads," you repeat. "They challenge you to make three treasures for the gods. Then the gods will decide whose work is best—yours or theirs."

"Bah!" says Brokk. "Don't listen to this deceiver. It's all a trick."

"No!" you say. "It's not a trick. I'll bet my head on it. If you make the best treasures for the gods, you shall have my head."

"You bet your head?" says Brokk. "We accept! We'll make three of the best treasures for the gods. Now get out of here, trickster."

Turn the page.

"This is perfect," you say as you leave the cave. "The golden hair is extraordinary. Nothing these blockheads make could possibly be better than that. There's no way I'll lose my head. Sif will get her golden hair, the gods will get new treasures, and everybody will love me."

You tighten the laces on your magic shoes to fly back to Asgard. Then you think of something and stop. "I wonder if I should make sure that Brokk and Eitri lose the challenge?"

To play a trick on Brock and Eitri, turn to page 31.
To fly back to Asgard, turn to page 33.

As the sons of Ivaldi finish the golden hair, they murmur magical spells over the strands. Then they drape the beautiful golden hair over your outstretched arms.

Your flying shoes bring you quickly back to Asgard. As you fly through the air, you hold the hair tightly under your cloak. This is a treasure you don't want to lose.

"I have the hair!" you announce to Thor and Sif. "And I must say, my trick turned out for the best—as all my tricks do. Sif, your hair was indeed beautiful before. But this hair is even more stunning."

When they see the golden hair, Thor and Sif are astounded. Without a word, Sif unties her headscarf and allows you to lift the hair to her bare skin. The hair magically attaches to her head like real hair.

Turn the page.

According to Norse myths, Sif's long golden hair flowed down her back like thick fields of grain.

Sif rushes to a mirror and runs her fingers through the brilliant, shimmering waves. The strands are light as snowflakes and shiny as sunlight on the water.

"You're right, Loki," says Thor. "She is even more beautiful than before." He gives you a friendly slap on the back. This time, it doesn't hurt.

THE END
To follow another path, turn to page 9.
To learn more about Thor and Loki, turn to page 103.

You fly back to Brokk and Eitri's cave. Using your power to transform, you change into a black fly. "Rather ugly," you say to yourself. "But it should work."

You buzz into the cave and see Brokk and Eitri working quickly. Brokk pumps air into the fire with a bellows while Eitri hammers some metal into shape. You can see that they've made a golden arm band. You also see a live, oinking boar with golden bristles.

Well, that's not very impressive, you think as you hover near the ceiling.

"This will be my masterwork," says Eitri. "I have planned this one for a long time. Make sure the fire stays hot."

Eitri puts a heavy block of iron into the blazing forge. Brokk keeps pumping the bellows to keep the fire roaring.

Turn the page.

Time to help out the brothers, you think, and fly down from the ceiling. You land on Brokk's sweaty forehead, right between his eyes. You lean over and take a chomp—right on his eyelid.

"Ow!" Brokk growls. He shakes his head, but you on hold tight. Then you scurry to the other eyebrow and take another chomp. Brokk stops pumping the bellows to swat at you, but misses.

Meanwhile, Eitri finishes hammering the last treasure for the gods and plunges the hot iron into water.

"Why did you stop pumping the bellows?" he yells at Brokk. "You almost ruined it. Who knows what the gods will say now?"

That's music to my ears, you think. You buzz out of the cave, change back to your normal form, and fly back to Asgard.

* * *

Days later in Asgard, all the gods have assembled for the contest. Odin the All-father sits on his throne. Thor sits on one side, and handsome Frey, god of the harvest, sits on the other.

You stand nearby, between the two teams of dwarves. They're ready to present their treasures to the gods.

You call for everyone's attention. "Today, we will learn who are the greatest craftsmen among the dwarves—the sons of Ivaldi or the brothers, Brokk and Eitri. They have made treasures worthy of the gods, and you—wise Odin, mighty Thor, and noble Frey—will decide which gifts are best."

You take the treasures from the sons of Ivaldi to present to the gods.

To Odin, you present a long, beautiful spear. "This is Gungnir," you announce. "It will always find its target, and its sharp tip will pierce anything."

Turn the page.

Odin holds the spear in both hands, and Thor and Frey lean over to look. They all admire the carved runes on the wooden shaft and the fine work of the spearhead.

To Frey, you present a silk scarf. "This is Skidbladnir," you say. "If you unfold this cloth, it becomes a great ship, bigger than any other. But you can fold it up and carry it in your pocket."

Odin and Thor nod their heads, impressed.

"And of course," you say, "the third treasure is worn by Thor's beautiful wife—Sif's flowing crown of golden hair."

The gods gasp in astonishment as Sif walks out before them. Her hair is brilliant in the sunshine. Odin grabs Thor's arm. "She is even more beautiful than before," says the All-father.

You look to Brokk and Eitri. A wide, gloating smile stretches across your face.

The two brothers then step forward to give their treasures to the gods. First, they present the boar with golden bristles to Frey.

The gods look confused. "This is Gullenbursti," says Brokk. "He'll pull your chariot across land, sea, or sky faster than any horse. And his golden bristles light up, so he can lead you at night."

The gods nod their heads in approval.

Uh, oh. This isn't good, you think.

"And for you, Odin," says Brokk, "we've made this golden arm band. It's called Dripper. Every ninth night it drips eight more gold bands just like it."

Odin looks impressed and right away pushes the arm band high on his bicep. You're feeling worried.

Turn the page.

"And lastly for Thor, we have this," Brokk says. Eitri steps forward and gives the god a hammer.

Thor looks disappointed. "The handle is quite short," he says. A smile curls on your lips.

"That was my brother's fault," says Eitri. "He didn't keep the forge hot enough. But the hammer is still remarkable. It will never break, it always hits its target when you throw it, and it will always return to your hand. It's called Mjölnir, the Lightning Maker."

Thor smiles as he picks up the hammer. "This hammer will help me to protect us from the frost giants," he says.

"But Thor," you interrupt, "what about Sif's beautiful hair?"

"Sure, her hair is nice," says Thor, staring at his hammer. "But this hammer is extraordinary."

The magical war hammer Mjölnir was highly prized by the god of thunder.

Odin and Frey also admire Mjölnir. "This hammer will protect all of Asgard," says Odin. "This is indeed the finest treasure."

Brokk and Eitri turn to you. "It's time to collect our prize," Brokk says. "We'll take your head now."

To run away from the dwarves, turn to page 38.
To talk your way out of the situation, turn to page 40.

Without saying a word, you dash off. You don't get far when something heavy hits your legs and knocks you down. When you look down, you see Thor's hammer tangled in your legs. Suddenly, Mjölnir whisks back to Thor's hand.

"It works!" Thor says. He picks you up and carries you back.

"You've lost the bet, Loki," says Odin. "Your head belongs to Brokk and Eitri." The gods all laugh to see you cornered. Thor's thick fingers grip your shoulder.

Thinking quickly, you transform yourself into a black fly again. You slip through Thor's fingers and fly out of his reach. Brokk and Eitri jump to grab you, but you zoom just above their hands.

With his one good eye, Odin spies you hovering above the gathering. "That is a good trick, Loki," he says. "But you can't stay a fly forever."

The gods and dwarves all laugh. You hate when your tricks turn out badly for you. But usually, everybody forgets—eventually. Besides, the gods like having you around, especially Thor. You'll just have to wait until this all blows over.

But in the meantime, you're stuck being a fly.

THE END

To follow another path, turn to page 9.
To learn more about Thor and Loki, turn to page 103.

"Yes, the brothers Brokk and Eitri have won the bet," you say. "And yes, I offered my head if they won."

The gods are all watching you in silence, wondering how you're going to talk your way out of this one.

"But . . ." you continue, "my neck was not part of the bet. To have my head, Brokk and Eitri need to cut my neck. And that breaks the deal."

Odin nods. "This is true," says the All-father. "The dwarves can't have his head without cutting his neck."

Brokk and Eitri look angry—and disappointed. "I have another idea," Brokk says. He motions toward Odin, and the god leans over as Brokk whispers in his ear.

"Yes," Odin says with a nod, "that will be fair. You will only be touching Loki's head."

You're worried as Brokk walks over to you. From his tool bag, he takes out a long needle and leather string.

"What are you doing?" you ask. "What's happening?"

"Stand still," says Brokk, "I'm only touching your head."

Brokk pierces the needle through your lips, up from the bottom, and out through the top. He pulls the thread through the holes. You grit your teeth in pain. Up and down, up and down, the dwarf slowly sews your mouth shut. Then he ties off the thread with a tight knot.

The gods and dwarves have a hearty laugh. You don't know what's worse—the pain of having your lips sewn shut or the pain of not being able to talk.

THE END

To follow another path, turn to page 9.
To learn more about Thor and Loki, turn to page 103.

With his magical war hammer, Mjölnir, Thor could summon and cast bolts of lightning at his enemies.

Chapter 3
Adventure in the Land of Ogres

You wake up with the sunrise, eager for a new adventure. You stretch out your arms and give Sif a kiss. "Goodbye, my love. I'll be home late."

You put on Megingjord, the Power Belt, which doubles your great strength. Then you slip on Jarngrieper, the Iron Gloves. You need them to hold Mjölnir. Then you look for your mighty war hammer, but Mjölnir is nowhere in sight.

"Maybe I left it in the banquet hall last night," you say. "Or maybe Loki knows where it is. He's usually to blame if something goes missing."

To search in the feasting hall, turn to page 44.
To question Loki about Mjölnir, turn to page 45.

Last night's feast was in Odin's great hall of Valhalla. This is where the All-father welcomes warriors from Midgard who have died heroically in combat. After their deaths, these warriors are brought to Valhalla by the Valkyries. These divine maidens watch over battles and decide who will live and who will die. You're proud that your daughter, Thrud, is one of the Valkyries.

This morning the hall is empty. The servants have cleared away the empty plates and goblets. You search everywhere for your powerful war hammer. You look under tables and chairs. You look behind the carved wooden pillars. You even search behind the beautiful tapestries on the walls. But there's no sign of Mjölnir.

Your hammer isn't here. And you know it isn't in your own chambers. You let out a growl. Loki must be up to one of his tricks. You decide to look for your mischievous friend.

You don't have to go far to find Loki. He's waiting by your chariot, ready for the day's adventure.

"Where's your hammer?" Loki asks. "Aren't we going on an adventure?"

"I don't know where it is," you answer. "What did you do with it?"

"I didn't do anything with it," Loki replies. "I do like to play tricks, especially on you, Thor. But I know enough not to touch Mjölnir. Do you want me to find out what happened?"

> To let Loki investigate while you eat breakfast, turn to page 46.
>
> To go with Loki to look for Mjölnir, turn to page 49.

"Yes, you go find out where Mjölnir went," you tell Loki. "I'll stay here and have my breakfast. I can't think straight on an empty stomach."

"You can count on me. I'll be back soon," Loki says and then dashes off.

As you turn to head for home, you murmur to yourself. "I can't let anyone know the hammer of the gods has been lost."

When you arrive back home, you push open the iron gate of your great hall, called Birskirnir. You wake your servants and tell them to get up and make your breakfast.

If the giants find out I don't have Mjölnir, they'll attack Asgard, you think as you tuck a napkin under your chin. Soon a mountain of bacon is placed before you, along with a hill of biscuits.

"Time for breakfast!" your sons shout. They rumble down the stairs in loud stomps. Magni and Modi look a lot like you. They're still too young to grow beards. But they're stronger than any of the gods, besides you.

They sit down and grab handfuls of bacon and biscuits. "Father, where is your hammer?" asks Modi.

"Oh, I left it upstairs in my chambers," you answer. Modi and Magni give each other puzzled looks. You never leave Mjölnir anywhere, even in your chambers.

Just then Loki bursts into the large hall. "Thor, I've found it!"

You jump from the table and slap your hand over Loki's mouth. "Loki, my friend!" you blurt. "Let's go outside and enjoy the morning sunshine."

Turn the page.

Outside the gate, you take your hand from Loki's mouth. "Now tell me . . . quietly," you say. "What did you learn?"

"Your hammer was stolen by Thrym, lord of the ogres," Loki explains. "I persuaded him to return it, but he demands a price."

"What does he want?" you ask.

"He wants to marry Freya," Loki says.

"Our Freya?" you ask. "Freya of Asgard? Freya, the goddess of beauty and love?"

"Yes, that Freya," Loki answers.

"Let's go talk to her," you say. "But you should do the talking. I don't think she'll like the idea, and you're better at persuading people."

Turn to page 53.

You and Loki stop first to visit Freya, the goddess of beauty and love.

"Will you lend us your feathered cloak, the one that can turn you into a falcon?" Loki asks. "Thor's hammer is missing, and we need to find it."

"Mjölnir is missing?" Freya answers. "Yes, you need to find it. Without the hammer, Thor can't protect us from the giants. You can use the cloak, but it will only turn one of you into a falcon."

You and Loki look at each other. "What do we do?" you ask. "I want to come with you to find my hammer. I miss it already."

"You use the cloak," Loki answers. "I'll use my power to transform into a small animal, one you can carry. A spiny hedgehog would be best. Then you won't be tempted to eat me."

Turn the page.

Freya brings you her feathered cloak. You wrap it around yourself, and you're instantly turned into a falcon. Loki changes himself into a hedgehog. Then you take him in your talons and fly off.

"We're looking for anything unusual," Loki tells you. "Then we'll stop and investigate."

A while later, you spot Thrym, lord of the ogres, sitting on a hill. He's making a dog collar.

That's looks pretty unusual, you think. You swoop down and turn yourselves back into Thor and Loki.

"I wondered when you would arrive," says Thrym. "I imagine you're looking for Thor's hammer."

"You have it?" you shout.

> To threaten to tear off the ogre's arms, go to page 51.
>
> To let Loki talk to the ogre, turn to page 52.

"Even without my hammer, I can rip any ogre apart!" you growl. "Tell me where my hammer is, or I'll tear off your arms!"

"I don't doubt that you can do that," says Thrym. "But then you won't have your hammer."

Loki interrupts. "He's probably right, Thor. You might not want to rip off his arms."

You grumble with disapproval. Thrym grins with ugly, crooked teeth.

"The hammer is hidden far underground," the ogre says. "It's safe there, until I get what I want."

"And what do you want?" you ask, your arms outstretched. "Gold? Silver? I can bring more treasure than you can imagine."

"I don't want treasure," Thrym says.

Turn the page.

Loki steps between you and the ogre lord. "What exactly is it that you want?" Loki asks.

"I want to marry Freya," says Thrym. "Bring her here a week from now. Then I'll return the hammer on our wedding day."

You and Loki look at each other and shrug your shoulders. You both turn back to Thrym and speak at the same time. "Freya will be here in a week."

You wrap the cloak around yourself and turn into a falcon again. Loki turns himself into a hedgehog. Once you're back in the air, you ask Loki how Freya will agree to marry an ogre.

"Leave that to me," Loki says slyly.

* * *

When Loki tells Freya the news, she gets so angry that the beams of her great hall start to quake.

"GET OUT!" she shouts. "Both of you! I'm not marrying an ogre!"

Freya slams the door behind you and Loki.

"We're going to need some help with this one," Loki admits. "Let's call the gods together."

The gods and goddesses gather quickly at Gladsheim, Odin's silver-roofed hall. All are there except Freya. She refuses to leave her house.

All afternoon and evening, the gods of Asgard debate what to do. All agree that Mjölnir must be returned, but nobody has an idea that will work.

"We need to stomp the ogres!" says your son Modi, flexing his biceps.

Turn the page.

"Modi's right!" adds Magni. "Father, the three of us together can get back your hammer."

"Yes, sons of Thor, we've heard from you already," says Odin. "There is only one here we have not heard from. Heimdall, what wisdom can you offer?"

Heimdall is the watcher of the gods. He stands guard at the far end of the Rainbow Bridge that connects Asgard to Midgard, the world of humans.

"I have an idea that might work," Heimdall says. "But I don't think Thor will like it."

> To go with your sons and smash the ogres, go to page 55.
>
> To listen to Heimdall's plan, turn to page 56.

"Come along, my sons," you announce, rising from your chair. "We'll go to Thrym and knock some sense into his head. He'll give us the hammer or face our fury."

Modi and Magni are already heading to the door. They've fought giants with you before.

"No, Thor!" Loki says, rushing to block your path. "You know this won't work. Thrym has hidden Mjölnir, and he won't give it back if you pound him. He wants Freya."

Then Heimdall holds up his hand. "With my plan, Thrym will get Freya, *and* you will get your hammer back," Heimdall says. "But you're not going to like it."

The room goes quiet. The gods and goddesses are surprised. Everyone leans in closer to hear Heimdall's idea.

Turn the page.

After Heimdall explains his plan, you fold your arms over your chest.

"You're right," you say with a grumpy huff. "I don't like this idea at all."

"I think it's a terrific idea," Loki says, grinning.

"You only think so because you like to see me humiliated," you tell Loki.

"No," Odin interrupts. "This is the best plan. Like Heimdall said, Thrym will get Freya. Then you'll get back Mjölnir, and we will all be safe."

You give Loki an angry look.

"Valkyries!" Odin calls out. The maidens who serve at Valhalla soon arrive and stand before the All-father.

"Take Thor away and get him ready. Dress him as a beautiful bride," Odin says with a smile. "He's going to the land of ogres to get married."

It takes a week to get you ready. The Valkyries sew a Thor-size wedding dress made of white silk and lace. They don't let you eat anything all week. Yet it still takes four Valkyrie maidens to stuff you inside the dress.

Finally, you're ready. Your wife, Sif, brings one of her golden necklaces and places it around your neck. Your daughter, Thrud, lowers a huge veil over your face. "There," she says. "Now nobody can see your face and beard."

Loki is waiting for you outside your hall. He's transformed himself into a young maiden, dressed in a beautiful gown. "I'm your bridesmaid," says the trickster. "Are you ready to go to your wedding?"

You grumble as you get into Freya's chariot. It's decorated with green ivy, red roses, and white ribbons. Loki steers the vehicle toward the land of the ogres.

Turn the page.

When you arrive, Thrym's hall is loud with music and laughter. The ogres cheer as you and Loki step carefully from the chariot in your long gowns. They even shower you with flower petals.

"I hope there's food at this wedding," you whisper to Loki. "The Valkyries didn't let me eat all week. I'm starving."

"You can't eat, Thor," Loki murmurs. "You eat so much they'll know it's a disguise."

You're disappointed, because inside the hall is a long table full of bottles of wine, pitchers of ale, and plates of cheese. Thrym is at the far end of the table.

"Welcome, my bride," he announces. "Please, Freya, sit here next to me."

"In Asgard, it is tradition that the bride and groom sit apart before the wedding," says Loki the bridesmaid. "I will sit between you."

"As you wish," Thrym says, stepping aside for you and Loki to sit down.

Loki leans over and whispers to you, "Remember, no eating."

Thrym calls for his servants. Soon there are platters of meat, fish, and vegetables on the table. Your mouth starts to water.

Just then you see it. Over there, on a table across the room, is your hammer!

> To rush across the room and grab Mjölnir, turn to page 60.
>
> To eat and satisfy your hunger first, turn to page 63.

Thor (left) was not pleased to be dressed as a bride. Meanwhile, Loki (right) enjoyed playing the trick on the ogres.

You lean toward Loki. "There's Mjölnir," you whisper intensely. "Over there, across the hall."

"I see it," Loki whispers back. "But there are six ogres guarding it."

"I can easily fight six ogres," you answer.

"Yes, but while you're fighting, they'll just hide the hammer again," Loki says. "Stick with the plan. Wait until they bring it to us."

"You just want me to be embarrassed in this wedding gown," you say.

Loki doesn't say anything. From beneath your veil, you look over to him. Loki the bridesmaid is enjoying a meal of cheese and goose wings.

You can't take it anymore. You throw back your chair and jump onto the banquet table. The ogres leap out of the way as you run to the other end of the table, stomping food and spilling drinks everywhere.

The ogre warriors are stunned to see Thrym's bride charge at them like a bull. They stand frozen in surprise. Before they figure out what's happening, you wallop them with your fists. You don't even smudge your wedding gown.

Turn the page.

You grab Mjölnir and turn to Loki. "I've got it!" you yell. But then you see that Thrym has Loki the bridesmaid in a headlock.

"My darling," says Thrym, "put down the hammer, and I won't hurt your bridesmaid."

"I'm no darling," you growl from beneath your veil. You hurl Mjölnir across the room. The hammer knocks the lord of the ogres to the floor and flies back to your hand. Loki dashes across the hall, still dressed in his gown.

"Let's get out of here!" Loki says. You rush outside to the chariot and speed away. The ogres chase behind you but can't keep up. The last thing they see is a runaway bride and bridesmaid, racing off with the hammer of the gods.

THE END

To follow another path, turn to page 9.
To learn more about Thor and Loki, turn to page 103.

Your stomach is rumbling at the sight and smells of the wedding feast.

"What's that noise?" Thrym asks. "It sounds like a bear growling."

"Oh, that's Freya's stomach," says Loki the bridesmaid. "She was so excited about the wedding that she hasn't eaten all week."

"Then she must have some of the cakes my servants made!" Thrym says. He waves his hand, and servants bring platters piled high with cakes filled with fruits, puddings, and minced meat.

As soon as the cakes are set before you, they disappear under your veil to the sounds of munching.

"She was certainly hungry," says Thrym. "Perhaps she would like some spring trout, caught in our streams."

Turn the page.

You eagerly watch the servants bring a huge platter full of cooked trout. One after another, you put the fish under your veil. Then you put each clean fish skeleton back on the platter.

"I have never seen a bride eat so much at her wedding," says Thrym.

"That's because she wants to match ogre women in strength," says Loki, thinking quickly. "It's only fitting that the great Thrym have a hardy wife."

"Then it's time for us to wed," Thrym declares. He slams a hand on the table. "Bring the hammer, so that its power will bless our marriage."

It takes all six ogre guards to carry Mjölnir. They set the hammer before you on the table.

"Let me hear your beautiful voice, my bride," says Thrym. "Put your hand on the hammer and speak our wedding vows. Tell me you will be my loving wife."

But instead of placing your hand on the hammer, you wrap your hand around Mjölnir's handle. You start to laugh.

"I have no vows to say. But I will tell you this," you growl. "You shouldn't have stolen my hammer."

In a flash, you tear off the veil and swing the hammer of the gods. Thrym and all the ogres fall beneath your fury. When the hall is silent, you finally rip yourself out of the wedding gown.

"Loki, where are you?" you call out.

Loki crawls out from under the banquet table. "Remind me to never take your hammer," he says, looking around at the destruction.

"Too bad we had to ruin my wedding," you say. "The ogres make a good feast."

THE END

To follow another path, turn to page 9.
To learn more about Thor and Loki, turn to page 103.

In Norse myths, Thor's chariot is pulled by two large goats named Grinder and Snarler.

Chapter 4
Journey to Giantland

"Good morning, Loki!" you say, looking up from preparing your chariot. "Are you ready for our adventure?"

"Indeed, I am," Loki replies. He points to the large sack that you've put on the chariot floor. "I see you've packed plenty of food, as always."

"You know how I am when I get hungry," you say. You finish tightening the reins on your two goats and give each of them a pat. They look stubborn, but they're strong and loyal.

"Everything is ready," you declare. "Shall we head to Utgard, the land of giants?"

"I'm ready for a new adventure," Loki answers. "Let's go."

Turn the page.

You steer the chariot over the Rainbow Bridge that connects Asgard to Midgard. You'll have to travel through the human world to reach Utgard.

It's a beautiful spring day in Midgard. The flowers are blooming, and leaves are budding on the trees. You and Loki have a pleasant day of traveling and talking. By the time the sun is low in the sky, you're at the far end of Midgard.

"There's a farmhouse ahead," Loki says. "Shall we stop for the night and finish our journey tomorrow?"

"That's a good idea," you answer. "Besides, I'm getting hungry. It will be good to have a hearty meal."

"What about the bag of food you packed?" Loki asks.

"We have a long journey ahead," you say. "We should save that for when we really need it."

When you reach the farm, the farmer, his wife, and their son are finishing their day's work. They're frightened to see the god of thunder roll up in his chariot.

"Do not fear," you tell them. "Loki and I will be your guests tonight. All we ask is a good supper—and a good breakfast, too. Then we'll be on our way in the morning."

"O, great and mighty Thor," the farmer pleads, "we have nothing to offer you. The winter has been hard, and our larder is empty. We have barely enough for ourselves."

"This is unfortunate," you say. Your stomach is just starting to rumble. You look back to Loki in the chariot. He gives a shrug. Then you look to your goats, Grinder and Snarler.

> To keep traveling, turn to page 70.
> To sacrifice your goats for dinner, turn to page 72.

"We'll not burden you, good people," you say to the farmer and his family. "When I return to Asgard, I'll ask the noble god Frey to give you an abundant harvest."

You and Loki climb back into the chariot and start away from the farmhouse.

"It's still a long way to Utgard," says Loki. "The land ahead is empty, only treeless marshes. How far will we travel before nightfall?"

"Grinder and Snarler do not tire," you reply. "We can keep going until we pass the marshes. Then we can find shelter in the woods."

After a short silence, you speak again. "However, I'm hungry now. Let's open the bag of food I brought."

"The bag is empty," Loki says.

"Nonsense," you say. "It was full of dried ox meat and biscuits with lard."

"I know," Loki says. "It was delicious."

"What?" you blurt. "You ate it all? When?"

"Back at the farmhouse. When you were talking to the farmer. I was hungry and looked in the sack. I took a bite, and then it was gone. You know how quickly I can eat."

You pull on the reins and turn the chariot around.

"What are you doing?" Loki asks. "I thought we were going to Giantland."

"We're going back to Asgard," you say. "You know how much I eat. If there's no food, there's no adventure."

THE END

To follow another path, turn to page 9.
To learn more about Thor and Loki, turn to page 103.

You turn back to the farmer. "If you have some vegetables for stew, I can provide the meat," you say.

"Thialfi," says the farmer's wife to their son, "bring some vegetables from the barn." Thialfi is a thin boy—perhaps fourteen or fifteen years old. He dashes off quickly. You can see that he moves fast.

"Loki, hand me Laeveteinn," you say. Laeveteinn is Loki's magic weapon. Just like Loki himself, it can change shape. Sometimes it's a spear, and sometimes it's a sword.

You use Laeveteinn as a knife. You walk up to your goats and plunge the blade into Grinder's neck. Then you do the same to Snarler. Neither goat struggles. Once they're dead, you cut the skin from both animals and bring the meat into the farmhouse kitchen.

"Here is the meat," you tell the farmer and his wife. "One for me, and one for the rest of you."

You spread out the two goat skins on the hearth. "After we eat the meat, the bones must be put on the goat skin. Be sure to put them all here. None can be broken or missing."

In a short time, the farmhouse fills with the smell of tasty stew. You and Loki, along with the farmer's family, squeeze together around a small table. You tell many tales as you eat. When everyone has had their fill, you put the bones on the goat skins. You put your bones on one skin while everyone else puts their bones on the other.

You sleep soundly that night by the fire.

* * *

When you wake the next morning, you wrap the bones in the goat skins and bring them outside. With Mjölnir raised above your head, a bolt of lightning flashes across the sky. Suddenly, the two goats stand up—alive and bleating! But then you see Grinder limping on a bad hind leg.

Turn the page.

"Who did it?" you roar. "Who disobeyed me? One of the goat's bones is broken."

The farmer and his wife clutch each other in terror. But their son steps forward bravely.

"I did it," Thialfi says, looking at his feet. "I broke the bone. We have gone so long without food, I broke the bone to suck out the marrow. I heard it would help me grow stronger."

"Oh, I see. I wonder where you might have heard that?" you say sarcastically, giving Loki a suspicious look.

"You may have been tricked, but you still need to repay me," you say to Thialfi. "You'll be our servant. The goats will stay here while Grinder's leg heals."

Leaving the chariot behind, you, Loki, and Thialfi set out on foot. Thialfi carries a pack filled with leftover vegetables and biscuits.

After walking most of the morning, you reach a long, narrow lake. It's surrounded by a thick forest. On the far side, you see the mountain of Utgard.

"Looks like we'll have to walk around the lake," you say. "But it's going to add another day to the journey."

"I think there's a faster way," says Loki, pointing across the lake. "Look. There's a boat on the other side. I think a forest troll is laying next to it."

>To get a ride on the boat, turn to page 76.
>To walk around the lake, turn to page 80.

"Hey over there!" you yell at the troll across the lake. The water ripples from the force of your voice.

The troll sits up and yells back. "Who are you? What do you want?"

"Bring your boat over!" you bellow. "We want to visit Utgard!"

The troll stands up. He's quite large, like forest trolls are. He puts on his hat and cups his hands around his mouth. "Why would I do that?" he yells.

You look at Loki. "Say that you'll pay him," Loki shrugs.

"We'll pay you!" you shout.

"I don't want your money!" the troll answers. "You're probably thieves running from trouble."

"We're not thieves!" you call back. "I'm Thor! And this is Loki! Ferry us across!"

"I know who Loki is!" the troll says. "But I've never heard of Thor!"

You look to Loki. "How does he not know who I am? Everybody knows who I am."

"Let me try," Loki says.

"This is Thor! The god of thunder! Son of Odin!" Loki shouts. "Come get us!"

"Never heard of him!" the troll responds. "Have him tell me a story! Maybe that will jog my memory!"

"Have you got a story to tell him?" Loki asks.

> To tell the story of Svarang's sons, turn to page 78.
>
> To tell the story of the sea hags, turn to page 79.

"I can tell you about the time I fought Svarang's sons!" you yell. "Do you know them?"

"Yes, they're a bunch of blockheads!" the troll yells. "But go ahead!"

"We were on opposite sides of the river, just like we are now!" you start. "They threw boulders at me! So, I threw one back . . . just like this!"

You pick up a large stone and hurl it over the lake. But the troll has to duck as the rock smashes through his boat.

"Now I remember you!" the troll calls. "You're a blockhead, too!"

You, Loki, and Thialfi turn around and trudge back to the farmhouse. "The troll is right, Thor," says Loki. "You really are a blockhead sometimes."

THE END

To follow another path, turn to page 9.
To learn more about Thor and Loki, turn to page 103.

"Let me tell you about the time I was on the island of Hlesey!" you start. "I fought the sea hags who lived there!"

"You fought women?" the troll shouts. "That's horrible!"

"They were sea hags!" you argue. "They were like serpents! With claws and fangs!"

"Doesn't matter!" yells the troll. "They were women! You can't go around fighting ladies! I'm not rowing over! You're a heartless brute!"

At that, the troll turns his back to you. Then he sits down and puts his fingers in his troll ears.

"I guess that's the end of this adventure," Loki says. "We'll just have to try again another day."

THE END

To follow another path, turn to page 9.
To learn more about Thor and Loki, turn to page 103.

"I don't want to get in a boat with a troll," you say. "Let's walk along the shore."

With Loki following behind, you clear a path through the thick pine forest. Thialfi runs ahead and then back, scouting the woods. Even carrying the full pack, he's swift as the wind.

As nightfall approaches, Thialfi returns with good news. "There's a meadow up ahead. And some kind of hut," he says.

"Good," you answer. "We can stop there for the night."

You and Loki are both puzzled by the hut. It has no door. Instead, one end is open as wide as the hut is high. You look inside. It is one large space, closed at the far end, with a small side room. The hut has no chairs, tables, beds, or windows.

"Strange place," you say. "But it should do for the night."

Thialfi starts a fire near the hut's entrance while you and Loki open the pack. There isn't enough to fill your stomachs, but the vegetables and biscuits take the edge off your hunger. After eating, you lie down near the entrance. Night hasn't fallen yet, but you're tired after the long day of walking. Loki falls asleep at the back of the hut, and Thialfi tucks himself in the side room.

You aren't asleep long before you're all jolted awake. The hut is shaking fiercely.

"It's an earthquake!" you shout, holding on to a wall.

The hut then lifts off the ground and rises into the air.

"What's happening?" Loki yells.

The hut turns on its side, and you all fall to the back. Out of the entrance, you can see the sky. Then the sky is blocked out—by a giant's face!

Turn the page.

The giant is startled to see you.

"What are you doing in there?" he asks. He lowers the hut and shakes you out onto the ground.

"I apologize," he says, as you brush off the pine needles. "If I had known you were sleeping in my mitten, I wouldn't have picked it up."

He's a polite giant, so you decide not to fight.

"We're on our way to Utgard," you say. "Can you lead us there?"

"My name is Skrymir," he replies. "Yes, we can go to Utgard. But it's nearly dark. We can rest here for the night, and then we can go tomorrow."

Skrymir lies down in the meadow and curls up like a baby. You, Loki, and Thialfi settle down nearby. The giant falls asleep and starts snoring—loudly. His snoring is so loud it shakes the trees. The three of you toss and turn in the grass, but no one can sleep.

"Thor, can you give him a little tap on the head with your hammer?" asks Loki. "Maybe that will knock him out enough to stop his snoring."

You agree and climb up onto Skrymir's huge head. Then you gently tap the side of his head with Mjölnir. Right away, he gets quiet. Maybe now you can get some sleep. You climb down and settle on the ground. The three of you soon fall asleep.

An hour passes, but then you're jolted awake. Skrymir is snoring again, louder than before. You decide to climb up to his head again and knock him harder with your hammer. He stops snoring, so you climb down again and fall back asleep.

But an hour later, you're awakened once again by Skrymir's loud snoring. Now you're mad. You climb the giant again and take a mighty swing with your hammer. Mjölnir sinks deep into his skull and bounces back.

Turn the page.

Skrymir was so large that even Thor could not harm the giant with his hammer.

The giant stops snoring and opens his sleepy eyes. "Did a leaf just fall on me?" he asks groggily. Then he closes his eyes and goes back to sleep.

"Hopefully that does the trick," you say to Loki and Thialfi. Thankfully, Skrymir sleeps peacefully until morning. You, Loki, and Thialfi finally get some sleep.

The next morning, you all start walking toward the mountain of Utgard. With his giant strides, Skrymir moves at the front. You and Loki can keep up, barely. But you're amazed at how quickly Thialfi can run.

As you get closer to Utgard, you see that it's not a mountain at all. It's an enormous fortress surrounded by a high wall. When you reach the huge iron gate, you see it's tall enough to even keep out a giant like Skrymir. He grips the bars and rattles them.

Turn the page.

"Strong as rock," he says, looking down at you, Loki, and Thialfi. "I'm going to continue on my journey. Enjoy your visit to Utgard." Then he strides off into the forest.

"How do we get in?" Loki asks.

Inside the gate is an empty courtyard. Beyond that, you can see the huge wooden doors of the great hall. You can hear laughter and music coming from inside. You try pulling and pushing on the bars, but they don't move.

"All together," you tell Loki and Thialfi.

"HEY!" the three of you yell together. "LET US IN!"

No one answers.

"What now?" Loki asks.

> To smash the gates open with your hammer, go to page 87.
>
> To climb over the gates, turn to page 90.

"Mjölnir will make easy work of these gates," you say. "Step back."

Loki and Thialfi give you room as you reach back with the hammer of the gods. With all of your might, you swing Mjölnir against the bars.

CLANG!

The hammer bounces back like a rubber ball.

"I thought your hammer could break anything," says Loki.

"That's what the dwarves who made it told me," you reply. You turn the hammer in your hand, examining its thick iron head.

You take another swing, this time with a fierce growl.

CLANG!

The bars don't even quake.

Turn the page.

"Maybe you can use it to pry the bars apart," Loki suggests.

You're willing to try anything. You wedge the head of Mjölnir between the bars and pull the handle back. The bars creak and bend, but just a little.

"I think I can get through now," says Thialfi. The boy turns sideways and slips between the bars.

"Maybe I can make it, too," suggests Loki. It's a tighter fit, but he squeezes through the gate.

You let go of Mjölnir's handle, and the bars snap back into place.

"What now?" you ask. "I can't fit through."

Loki and Thialfi go to the door of the great hall. They pound and yell, but no one answers. They jump to reach the door handle, but it's too high above their heads.

They come back to the gate to find you pulling, prying, and hitting the gate with your hammer. But the bars won't budge.

"It's no use," you admit. You pry open the bars for Thialfi and Loki to squeeze back outside.

You look back through the bars at the great hall. You can still hear the music and laughter. You also hear plates of food rattling and huge tankards of ale clanking together.

"I can't believe it. Locked out of a great feast," you say sadly. "Let's go back. I'm getting hungry."

THE END

To follow another path, turn to page 9.
To learn more about Thor and Loki, turn to page 103.

You try pulling on the iron bars again, but they don't budge. You look up to see the top of the gate far overhead.

"We could try climbing over the top," you say.

"You go first," Loki says. "We'll follow behind."

You spit in your hands and rub your palms together. Then you grab hold of the bars and start climbing.

"This isn't bad," you say. "It's just like the time I fought the giant Geirrod. We had to climb a cliff to reach his castle. That was harder than this."

Loki doesn't answer.

He must be too tired to talk, you think to yourself. *He's not in the best shape.*

At the top, you swing your legs over the gate and slide down to the ground below. When you land, Loki and Thialfi are waiting on the inside.

"We squeezed under the gate instead," Loki says with a smirk. "Even you could have fit, Thor."

You glare at Loki with a huff. Then you move to the huge wooden door and pound on it with your hammer. The door swings open, and you enter the vast hall.

Inside you find giants sitting at huge tables. These are the biggest giants you have ever seen. They stop their feasting and laughing and watch you walk down the center of the room.

"Thor, son of Odin," booms a voice from the far end of the hall. You see the Giant King seated on the highest chair. "Welcome to Utgard."

The Giant King appears handsome and wise. You've never seen such an impressive giant.

"And this must be Loki," the king says. "We've heard so much about you both. But . . . you're kind of small for gods."

Turn the page.

The giants start laughing, until the king holds up a hand for silence. "Utgard offers great treasure, for those of great talent," he says. "Can any of you impress us with a unique feat?"

You huddle with Loki and Thialfi. "I can show them a feat of strength," you say.

"You couldn't open the gates," Loki says. "I think your strength won't go far here. I can show them how quickly I eat. They've never seen anything like that."

Thialfi interrupts. "I can show them my speed. I kept up with Skrymir in the forest. I can surely beat a giant in a race."

> To show the giants a feat of strength, go to page 93.
>
> To have Loki show how fast he can eat, turn to page 95.
>
> To have Thialfi challenge a giant in a race, turn to page 97.

"You have heard of the great strength of Thor," you declare. "I challenge anyone here who is brave enough to wrestle me in a match."

"You're quite small," the king remarks. "I don't think it would be fair to wrestle one of us. But you can wrestle Ellie, my old nanny. She taught me to wrestle when I was a boy."

The guests laugh as an old lady giant hobbles forward. You're furious at the idea of wrestling an old woman. But then Ellie throws away her walking stick and gets into a fighting stance.

You hurl yourself at her, but she's like a rock wall. You grapple together until she throws you off balance and forces you to your knees. The giants all laugh.

"We've seen enough, Thor," the king declares. "You're not strong enough to defeat my old nanny. The treasures of Utgard are not for you."

Turn the page.

The king rises and points to the door. "You can take your leave, along with your companions."

You turn to walk out, hanging your head in anger and shame.

"Don't be too disappointed, Thor," says the king. You turn back. "You see, Ellie isn't really a giant. She represents old age, which nobody can defeat. In the end, old age comes for us all. Even we giants cannot defeat her."

At that, the king says goodbye, and the door of the great hall closes behind you as you leave. You begin your long trip back to Asgard. It wasn't much of an adventure, but you've learned a wise lesson about life.

THE END

To follow another path, turn to page 9.
To learn more about Thor and Loki, turn to page 103.

"No one in this hall can eat faster than me," Loki declares.

"I'd like to see this," the king answers. "My servant can eat quickly. Let's see how you match up against him."

Two round tables are brought in before the king. Each is filled with roasted chicken, sheep, rabbits, and oxen. Loki stands before one table, the king's servant before the other. The king slaps his hands, and they both begin eating.

Loki eats so quickly that you can't see his hands. In just seconds, he looks up and wipes his mouth. Loki looks over to the king's servant. He's done eating, too. But he has eaten everything, including the meat, the bones—even the tabletop. The table legs lay sprawled on the floor.

"You do eat quickly, Loki," says the king. "But you can't eat as much as my servant."

Turn the page.

The king calls for the kitchen workers. They bring out three sacks bursting with food. They set the sacks before you, Loki, and Thialfi.

"You've performed well, so I'm providing you with enough dried meat and biscuits for your return journey," the king says. "But now you must leave. Utgard is not for you."

You start toward the door before the king calls again. "Wait. Since you are a trickster, Loki, you'll enjoy this," he says. "You see, my servant was fire, and fire can devour everything—including the meat, bones, and even the table. You are indeed a fast eater. But fire can eat much more."

As you leave, Loki has a satisfied smile on his face. He loves a good trick, even when it's played on him.

THE END

To follow another path, turn to page 9.
To learn more about Thor and Loki, turn to page 103.

"This is my servant, Thialfi," you announce. "He is just a boy, but he can match any giant in a footrace."

"That would indeed be a unique feat," says the Giant King. "Let's go outside. We'll see if this boy can match a giant's speed."

Outside the fortress is a flat, grassy space. The king calls upon a young giant named Hugi.

"Here is your challenger," the king says to Thialfi.

The young giant and the boy stand side by side at the starting line. The king gives a signal, and they take off running. They both run so fast, it seems their feet don't touch the ground. Thialfi stays close for half the course, but then Hugi pulls ahead and beats him easily. The giants cheer, not only for Hugi, but also for Thialfi.

Turn the page.

"I must say," the king declares, "I never imagined that a boy from Midgard could perform such a feat. That was truly unique. You are all welcome to feast at my table."

You all follow the king back into the hall, along with the other giants. At last, you're able to eat your fill. You feast on baked salmon, roasted deer, and broiled duck. After the long journey, you eat eagerly.

"I will make a confession," the Giant King says. "I have played a trick on the three of you."

"What trick is that?" you ask.

"Thor, earlier I used my magic to take away a bit of your strength," says the king. "That's why you couldn't move the fortress gates."

You feel your anger rising. You don't like being tricked—not by Loki, and certainly not by a strange giant.

"And Thialfi, I took away a bit of your speed," the king continues. "That's why you lost to Hugi."

"When did you do this?" asks Loki. "I didn't see you cast a spell on us."

"I cast my spell last night," the king explains. "When you were inside my mitten."

"Wait, you were Skrymir?" you ask.

"Yes, that was my disguise," says the Giant King. "That's why your hammer blows didn't kill me, Thor. Mjölnir bounced off my skull thanks to my magic."

Now you're mad. You don't like having secret spells placed on you by giants who pretend to act politely.

You grip the handle of Mjölnir and lift the hammer over your head. You're ready to destroy this fortress and this deceiving Giant King.

Turn the page.

Thor, Loki, and Thialfi learned that Castle Utgard was not a castle at all. It was another masterful illusion created by the Giant King.

But before you can swing the hammer, the king disappears. The giants also disappear. Even the walls and tables of Utgard fade away like mist.

Loki begins to clap. "Oh, that was brilliant," he says. "A perfect illusion."

You don't share his appreciation of the trick. But you have no way to show your anger. You stand with your hammer in an empty field.

"We came all this way for nothing," you complain to Loki.

"I would disagree. We have an amazing story to tell everyone back in Asgard," Loki says. "And young Thialfi here can tell his family about our adventure, too."

"But we have nothing to show for it," you protest. "No gold. No treasure. Nothing to prove the story is true."

"Dear Thor, don't you know? That's the best kind of story," Loki says.

"Come on," he adds, slapping you on the back. "Let's share our story with everyone back home. They'll love it!"

THE END

To follow another path, turn to page 9.
To learn more about Thor and Loki, turn to page 103.

A Norse temple at Uppsala in Sweden featured statues of Odin, Thor, and Frey. Nordic people worshipped and honored the gods with many sacrifices at the temple.

Chapter 5
The God of Thunder and the Trickster

Most religions have moral lessons that teach the difference between good and evil. But the religious beliefs of the ancient Norse people didn't do that.

In Norse mythology, Thor is not a model of goodness or kindness. And Loki isn't Thor's enemy or an evil being. Instead of good and evil, Thor and Loki are models of two other ideas: order and chaos.

For the ancient Norse people of Scandinavia, order called for all people to be loyal to their king. Children had to obey their parents. And servants had to work for their masters.

Order also extended to the natural world. It meant that the rains would come in the spring, and the sun would shine in the summer. This allowed crops to grow, and people could harvest them in the fall.

Chaos was also all around in nature. It could disrupt life for the Norse people at any time. A terrible hailstorm could ruin the crops in the field. Or wolves could kill a family's sheep.

But chaos wasn't always considered to be bad. A king needed loyal warriors. But he also needed them to be fierce in battle.

Today the word "berserk" often describes someone who is acting out of control. The word comes from the ancient Norse word *berserkir*, or berserker. These were warriors who fought fiercely and in an out-of-control way. In battle, they fought like crazed bears to scare and overwhelm their enemies.

Berserkers often wore the skins of bears, wolves, or other animals in battle. They believed the spirits of the animals helped them to fight more fiercely.

The stories of Thor and Loki taught the ancient Norse people that a balance of order and chaos was needed in life. Thor's ferocious anger often resembled how berserkers fought in battle. He was a mighty warrior but sometimes got out of control. Loki's tricks helped to keep Thor's anger in check and to restore balance and order to the world.

Norse Family Tree

Loki and Thor weren't brothers. Thor was a god, the son of Odin. Loki's father was a giant, and his mother a goddess. Odin tried to make Loki his blood brother to keep him on the side of the gods. But it didn't work. At the battle of Ragnarök, Loki and his own children turned against the gods and helped bring the end of the world in Norse mythology.

THOR'S FAMILY TREE

ODIN
The All-father, the creator of the nine worlds, father to many gods, and the god of wisdom and battle. If a warrior lived a good life and died heroically, that person would go to the great hall of Valhalla to feast forever with Odin.

JÖRD
Thor's mother, the goddess of Earth

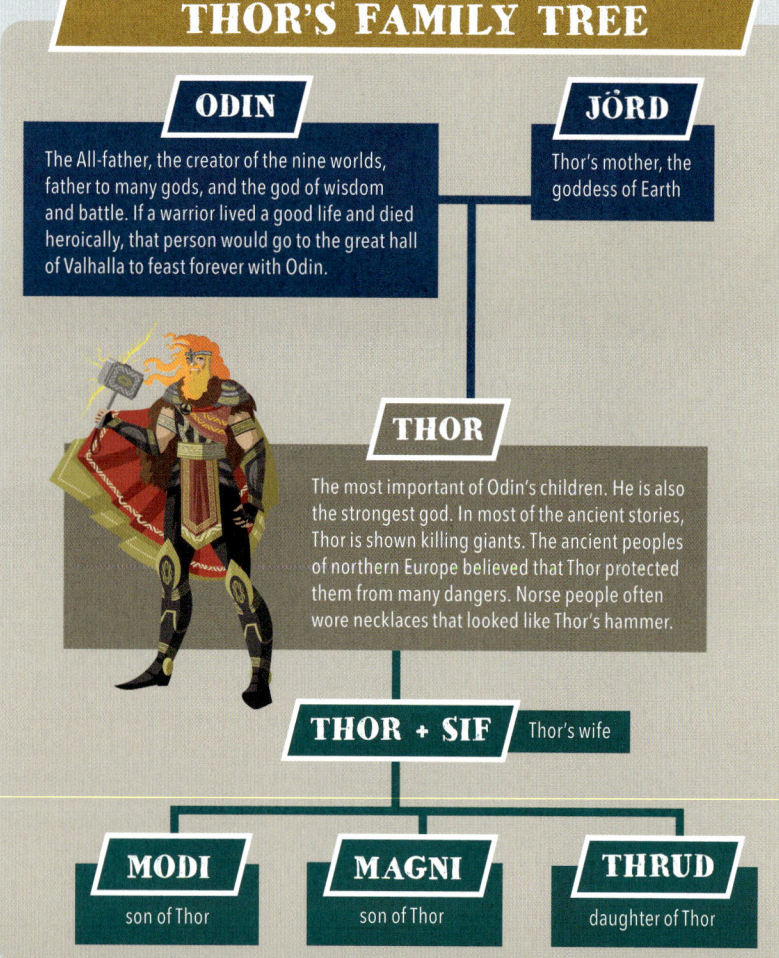

THOR
The most important of Odin's children. He is also the strongest god. In most of the ancient stories, Thor is shown killing giants. The ancient peoples of northern Europe believed that Thor protected them from many dangers. Norse people often wore necklaces that looked like Thor's hammer.

THOR + SIF
Thor's wife

- **MODI** — son of Thor
- **MAGNI** — son of Thor
- **THRUD** — daughter of Thor

LOKI'S FAMILY TREE

FARBAUTI
Loki's father, a giant

LAUFEY
Loki's mother, a goddess

LOKI
Wasn't actually a god, but a giant. He wasn't always a villain. In many stories, he traveled with Thor on his adventures. But he often played tricks on the gods. One of his tricks led to the death of Thor's brother Baldur, who was one of the most beloved of all the gods.

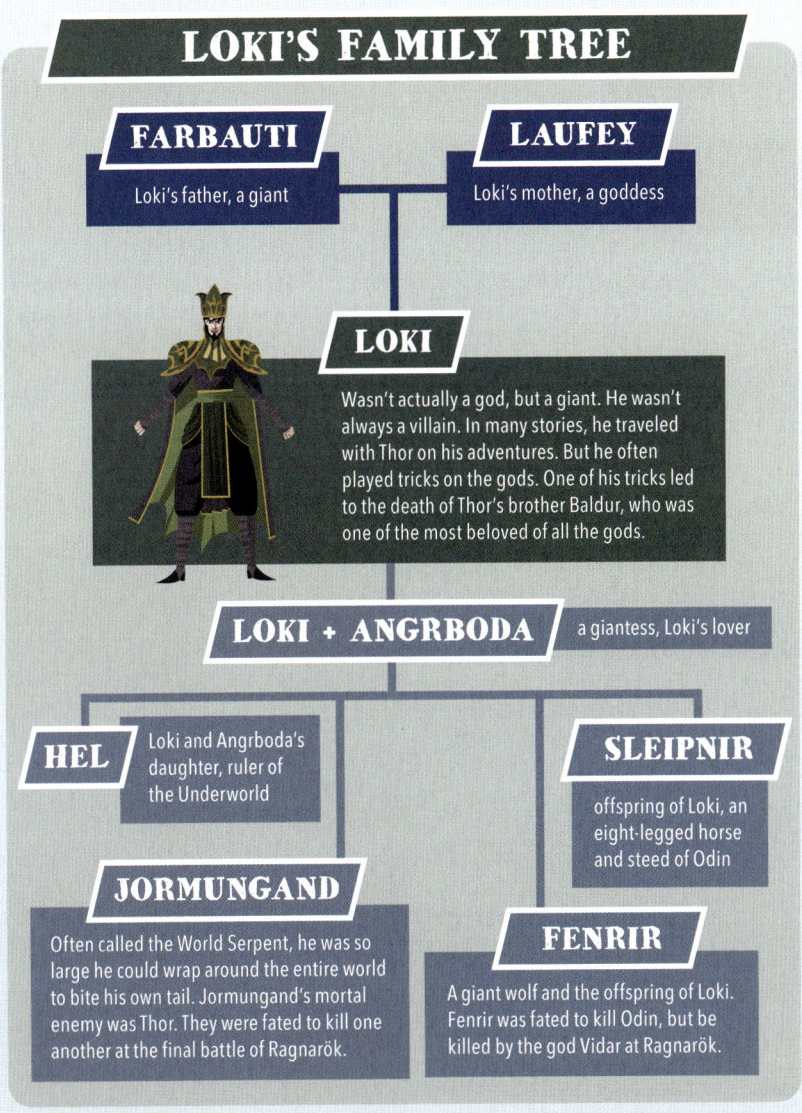

LOKI + ANGRBODA
a giantess, Loki's lover

HEL
Loki and Angrboda's daughter, ruler of the Underworld

SLEIPNIR
offspring of Loki, an eight-legged horse and steed of Odin

JORMUNGAND
Often called the World Serpent, he was so large he could wrap around the entire world to bite his own tail. Jormungand's mortal enemy was Thor. They were fated to kill one another at the final battle of Ragnarök.

FENRIR
A giant wolf and the offspring of Loki. Fenrir was fated to kill Odin, but be killed by the god Vidar at Ragnarök.

At Ragnarök, Loki brought an army of dead warriors from the Underworld to fight the gods. The wolf Fenrir fought Odin and Frey, and Jormungand fought Thor. Almost all the gods and monstrous creatures from Norse myths died in the final battle.

Other Paths to Explore

>>> In the stories of Loki and Thor, Loki isn't Thor's enemy. Despite Loki's tricks, Thor still likes to travel with and share adventures with Loki. Do you know someone who causes mischief but is still fun to have around? Why do you think people enjoy having a trickster as a friend? Try writing a story about this person and how they almost got in trouble for their actions.

>>> Thor was known as the strongest of the gods. Loki could change his form and disguise himself to play tricks on others. Which of these superhuman abilities would you like to have? How would you use that ability? Would you use your powers to help others or use them to play pranks?

>>> In later stories from Norse mythology, Loki goes too far with his tricks. One of the gods dies as a result of his pranks, and the gods punish him. We all like to joke and have fun with our friends and family. But sometimes tricks, pranks, or jokes can hurt others. Can you think of a time when you or someone you know got hurt because of another person's tricks?

Bibliography

Crossley-Holland, Kevin. *The Norse Myths*. New York: Pantheon Books, 1980.

Gaiman, Neil. *Norse Mythology*. New York: Norton, 2017.

Lindow, John. *Handbook of Norse Mythology*. Santa Barbara, CA: ABC-CLIO, 2001.

Norse Mythology for Smart People. https://norse-mythology.org/

Glossary

bellows (BEH-lohz)—an air bag with two handles used to blow air into a stove or furnace to make a fire burn at high temperatures

divine (dih-VINE)—holy or sacred; related to godlike or supernatural beings

forge (FOHRJ)—a special furnace in which metal is heated before shaping it

larder (LAHR-der)—a room or place where food is kept

marrow (MAYR-oh)—the soft substance inside bones where blood cells are made

rune (ROON)—a symbol in the alphabet of ancient Northern Europe

Scandinavia (skan-duh-NAY-vee-uh)—the area of northern Europe that includes Norway, Denmark, and Sweden

tankard (TANG-kerd)—a large drinking cup, usually with a handle and a hinged cover

Valhalla (vahl-HAH-luh)—in Norse mythology, the great hall of Odin where the souls of heroes killed in battle and others who died bravely go after death

Valkyrie (val-KEER-ee)—in Norse mythology, female helpers who serve Odin and bring slain warriors from the battlefield to Valhalla

Read More

Bowen, Carl, Michael Dahl, and Louise Simonson. *Gods and Thunder: A Graphic Novel of Old Norse Myths*. North Mankato, MN: Capstone Young Readers, 2017.

Nordvig, Mathias. *Norse Mythology for Kids: Tales of Gods, Creatures, and Quests*. Emeryville, CA: Rockridge Press, 2020.

Ralphs, Matt. *Norse Myths*. New York: DK Publishing, 2021.

Internet Sites

Kiddle: Norse Mythology Facts for Kids
kids.kiddle.co/Norse_mythology#Cosmology

Thor and Loki in the Giant's City
dltk-kids.com/world/norway/children-of-odin/thor-and-loki.htm

The Vikings: Gods and Myths
vikings.mrdonn.org/gods.html

About the Author

Bruce Berglund is a writer and historian. For two decades, he taught world history courses to college students. He has traveled in Europe, Asia, and South America. When he visited Iceland, he learned that Thor is a popular name there. Bruce grew up in Duluth, Minnesota, so he knows what it's like to live through the Mighty Winter.

Photo Credits
Alamy: Chronicle, 6, Danvis Collection, 30, Ivy Close Images., 102, Michelle Bridges, 14, Wirestock, Inc., 37; Bridgeman Images: Look and Learn, 84; Getty Images: fotokostic, Cover, 42; Shutterstock: bluelake, 19, delcarmat, 10, Larry Jacobsen, 100, Liliya Butenko, 66, Warm_Tail, 105; Wikimedia: Carl Larsson/Gunnar Forssell, 60